D1133921

THE CATHEDRAL IN HISTORY

After the fall of the Roman Empire in the fifth century Kent fell under Saxon domination and the King of Kent had his capital in the old Roman city of "Durovernum Cantiacorum". To this place, the "Canterbury" of the Middle Ages and of Modern times, came monk missionaries from Rome in 597 invited by the King, Ethelbert, and his Frankish Christian Queen, Bertha. The success of their mission and the conversion of the King and many of his subjects led to the consecration of Augustine, leader of the mission, as Archbishop, with his base at Canterbury, and the establishment of a church in which he could set up his "Cathedra", or official seat, in what is now the Precincts.

The Church has always been the seat of the Archbishops of Canterbury from the time of Saint Augustine. The Norman Conquest saw the rebuilding, after a fire in 1067, of the Cathedral on a magnificent scale, worthy of what was by this time a great Benedictine monastic community. The martyrdom of Saint Thomas in 1170 led to it becoming the greatest pilgrimage church in northern Europe. Another fire in 1174 made the rebuilding of the monks' quire a necessity and this emerged as the first major building in England in the Gothic style. The rebuilding of the nave and cloisters in the Perpendicular Gothic style (14th century) and the reconstruction of the towers and transepts in the following century ensured that at the end of the Middle Ages, when the shrine of Thomas Becket was destroyed and the monastery dissolved, Canterbury Cathedral was one of the noblest churches in Christendom.

Today its role as a pilgrimage church is rather different from the mediaeval concept, but for many millions it is the Mother Church of the Anglican Communion and a place where the dignity of worship, both musically and liturgically, attracts multitudes of faithful believers (as well as many tourists). It is the earnest desire of the Dean and Canons of the Chapter to whom the ongoing life of the Cathedral is entrusted that those who come with great expectations shall have them amply fulfilled and as they go shall say indeed, "This is none other than the House of God, and this the Gate of Heaven".

ARRIVING AT THE CATHEDRAL

The visitor to the Cathedral will normally approach the city along Mercery Lane to enter the Precincts by way of the **Christ Church Gate**, a structure of early Tudor period, thought to have been built as a memorial to Henry VII's eldest son Arthur, Prince of Wales, who died at the age of 16 in 1502.

The many coloured shields of arms carved on it represent officers of his household and trusted supporters of Henry VII. The modern figure of the welcoming Christ replaces the original which was pulled down by the Puritans in 1642. It was sculpted by Klaus Ringwald in 1990 and was given by the Friends of the Cathedral.

Passing under the gate with its heavy wooden doors, given by Archbishop Juxon in 1663, the great church, 514 feet in length, lies before us. At once we can see the rich variety of architectural styles that make this such a fascinating building.

The western towers and nave are clearly late Middle Ages (late 14th and early 15th century) while the quire, beyond the western transept, is an early Gothic structure of late 12th century built upon a Romanesque crypt some seventy years older; the whole church being linked into one by the towering bulk of the central (Bell Harry) tower rising to 235 feet and completed in 1498. The statues in the south-west porch are of mid-Victorian era, representing characters in the history of the Cathedral.

The South West Porch

1 THE NAVE

Enter the Cathedral at the south-west porch main entrance, built in the reign of Henry V. Just inside the south door is a figure of Christ in afromosia wood, with open arms welcoming the visitor. Above in the tower is the Cathedral ring of 14 bells while in the north-west tower, rebuilt in the Gothic style in 1832, hangs Great Dunstan (62 cwt) and the clock chimes.

Inside the Nave, in the arcade near the north door stands the Font, a fine work of the Stuart period given by Bishop Warner of Rochester in 1639. It is made of marble with figures of the Four Evangelists round the base and the Twelve Apostles on the cover, which is lifted by a system of pulleys. It is said to have been smashed in 1642 by the Puritans and repaired after the Restoration of 1660 having been preserved in secret by William Somner, the Antiquary, during the Commonwealth.

In the chapel of Saint Augustine, under the north-west tower, beneath his mock gothic monument, lies Archbishop Benson, the only Archbishop buried in the Cathedral since Tudor times. The subject of the large window above the chapel altar is the sending of Augustine to England, showing Pope Gregory I above and the Archbishop beneath. Below the window is a full list of the Archbishops.

The Nave Pulpit

The **pulpit** (1898) is a fine wooden one carved and painted, a memorial to Dean Payne-Smith, designed by Mr G C Bodley. Standing in the middle of the Nave one can look up to see the rich lierne vaulting above one's head and the many coats of arms in stone which may commemorate donors to the fabric fund of the 14th century.

The Nave

The visitor will be conscious of the large number of memorial tablets that encrust the walls of the side aisles. They are mainly of a military character. On the north wall is the **nave organ** given by Lord Astor of Hever in 1980, and close by, a fine portrait bust by Nicholas Stone of the great English composer, Orlando Gibbons, who died in Canterbury on his way out of the morning service in the Cathedral on Whitsunday 1625, while awaiting the arrival of Charles I and his French bride, Queen Henrietta Maria.

The Compass Rose is the symbol of the worldwide communion of the Anglican Church. The Greek inscription is translated "The truth will set you free" (John 8 v32). The brass was inserted in the floor to mark the end of the 1988 Lambeth Conference and marks the Cathedral as the mother church of the Anglican Communion.

The Compass Rose

Across the building from north to south runs an elaborately fretted 'strainer arch' inserted with the other strainers c1500 to distribute the weight of the tower. Behind the Nave altar rises a flight of steps leading to the quire. On these stands the **Pulpitum screen,** dividing the quire from the Nave, known as the Screen of the Six Kings because of the 15th century crowned figures which fill the niches on its facade. On top of the screen is the console of the **Cathedral organ,** built by Henry Willis in 1886, since when it has undergone several alterations up until 1979 when it was completely rebuilt by Noel Mander.

The Pulpitum Screen

2 THE WEST WINDOW

Turn and face the west window at the end of the Nave. This contains 13 figures from the genealogy of Christ dating from the late 12th century and brought here from the clerestory of the quire in 1797. In the centre of the bottom row is a figure of Adam Delving after the expulsion from Eden, one of the oldest pieces of glass in this country. Above these patriarchal figures are eight kings belonging to the mid 15th century and in the tracery above the apostles and the saints, c1400.

Adam Delving, West Window

The Martyrdom

3 THE MARTYRDOM TRANSEPT

Descending the steps on the left into the north-west transept we find ourselves standing near the spot where the tragic death of **Saint Thomas Becket,** Archbishop and Martyr, took place at dusk on the winter evening of December 29th 1170. The knights burst in through the cloister door as he was about to go up to Vespers and killed Thomas at once on the pavement, just inside the door.

From that day this has been a hallowed spot and place of pilgrimage. Here came Pope John Paul II and Archbishop Robert Runcie to pray together on May 29th 1982 and here has been placed a modern version of the **'Altar of Sword's Point'** to which medieval pilgrims came for so many centuries.

Under the great Royal window are tombs of two arch-bishops, Peckham (1294) and William Warham (1553) while over the Cloister door is a modern window of 1954 by Comper with figures of royal and other personages who took part in the coronation ceremonies of 1937 and 1953, including Queen Elizabeth II as a princess.

Through a beautiful stone screen lies the Chapel of **Our lady Martyrdom,** with a fan vault, built in the mid 15th century. It is sometimes known as the Deans' Chapel because of the numerous monuments of deans of the 16th and 17th centuries that it contains. The chapel has a contemporary east window enriched with 15th century heraldry together with a tapestry, a statue of the Virgin and Child, and a hanging pyx, all by artists of our own time.

4 THE WESTERN CRYPT (We ask our visitors to proceed in silence in the crypt)

We now descend a flight of steps and pass through a doorway, the style of which gives an indication of what is to come.

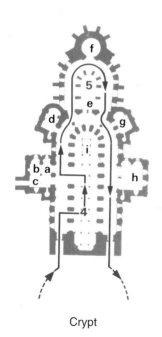

a. Chapel of St. Nicholas

b. Chapel of St. Mary Magdalene

c. North door of Crypt leading to Water-tower

d. Chapel of the Holy Innocents

e. Site of Becket's Tomb from 1170 until 1220

f. Jesus Chapel

g. Chapel of St. Gabriel

h. The Black Prince's Chantry (now the Huguenot church)

i. Chapel of Our Lady of the Undercroft

Crypt

The great Romanesque crypt was built in the first years of the 12th century. Standing at the west end we have behind us a wall which belongs to the time of Archbishop Lanfranc who was responsible for building the Romanesque Cathedral c1077. This is now enclosed in the **Treasury** which contains not only church plate, belonging both to the Archbishopric and the Cathedral Chapter, but also many pieces from the parishes of the Diocese of Canterbury.

Looking east we see a forest of columns with shafts and capitals, alternately carved and plain; some of the finest Romanesque carving in England. At the far end is the Sanctuary of **Our Lady Undercroft,** surrounded by rich 14th century screens of carved and painted stone with a modern bronze statue of Madonna and Child set over the altar.

In the north transept are the altars of **Saint Nicholas** and **Saint Mary Magdalene** while in the opposite side is the **Black Prince's Chantry** used by the Huguenot community as their church; every Sunday afternoon at 3 pm worship is offered here to God in French.

The Western Crypt

Two eastern chapels include on the north side **Holy Innocents** with richly carved pillars supporting the roof and on the south side the chapel of **Saint Gabriel** with 12th century paintings on the walls and vault, showing scenes in which angels appear. A modern icon of the Annunciation and a pillar carved with dancing animals, contemporary with those in the main Crypt, complete the ensemble.

5. THE EASTERN CRYPT

Behind the chapel of Our Lady Undercroft is the place where Saint Thomas was first buried and where Henry II performed his penance. On September 5th 1174 a great fire destroyed the Quire above, only some forty years after dedication. In the rebuilding that followed, this eastern crypt, which we now enter, was added to the church as an undercroft for the Trinity Chapel above, which was to become the shrine of the saint and to provide adequate space for the multitude of pilgrims who were streaming down to Canterbury.

The body of Thomas Becket lay in this area of the Crypt from the time of the Martyrdom in 1170 to the Translation of the body in 1220, and many miracles of healing are thought to have taken place here. At the west end, high up under the altar above, was constructed a **watching chamber** where the monks could keep guard over the tomb below.

The crypt terminates in the lovely **Jesus Chapel** with rich early glass in its centre window and Gothic vault and letters M and I crowned (for Mary and Jesus) between the ribs. A curious scratching of the 13th century behind the clergy stalls shows the figure of Jesus among the symbols of the four evangelists.

6 THE WARRIORS' CHAPEL OF SAINT MICHAEL

Leaving the crypt by the south door a modern window by Christopher Whall faces us in the west wall of the transept. Dating from 1903 it shows the Birth of Christ with the Agony in the Garden and the Resurrection above. Opposite is the ship's bell of HMS Canterbury. It is struck daily at 11 am as a commemoration of the fallen of the World Wars.

In the chapel the old colours of the Buffs (Royal East Kent) Regiment are laid up. The modern east window by William Wilson and the altar with its cross and candlesticks are memorials to the men of the regiment, as is the reredos under which lies one of the greatest of

Archbishops, Cardinal Stephen Langton. He was buried in 1228 in a simple stone coffin, the end of which protrudes oddly into the churchyard.

The chapel is dominated by a huge tomb on which lie effigies of three royal personages. In the centre Lady Margaret Holland, with, on her left, her first husband, John Beaufort, Earl of Somerset, and on her right, her second husband, Prince Thomas Plantagenet, Duke of Clarence. She had the old Norman chapel rebuilt just before she died in 1439; all around lie warrior figures of the Stuart period.

The Warriors' Chapel

A massive tablet commemorates Sir George Rooke, a local worthy, who was Admiral in command of the British fleet which captured Gibraltar in 1793.

7 UNDER THE TOWER

Walking up the steps from the transept to look down the nave, we gaze up into the lantern of the great **central tower** (known as Bell Harry from the curfew bell on its summit). The fan vault has carved on it the arms of those responsible for its erection. Chief among these were Cardinal John Morton and the Prior Thomas Goldstone II whose united efforts in raising funds and securing the services of a great architect, John Wastell, have given us one of the noblest towers in existence.

The vaulting of Bell Harry Tower

Begun in 1494 and finished ten years later, it is composed of some 480,000 bricks covered with a skin of stone. The interior is carved with various devices of Cardinal Morton, trusted minister of King Henry VII, whose arms are also on the vaulting. Turning north we can see from here the great **Royal window** of the martyrdom inserted c1480 with pictures in glass of the Yorkist king, Edward IV, his wife and family which includes his daughter, Elizabeth (wife of Henry VII), her sisters and the two tragic princes murdered in the Tower. The tracery is still filled with many charming figures of saints but the main lights were wrecked by Puritan fanaticism in 1642.

Turning and looking across the south-west transept we can see a galaxy of patriarchal figures . . . 24 in all . . . dating from the years 1178 -1190, all brought there from the clerestory of the quire in 1793. Part of a series showing the genealogy of Christ they include figures of Noah, Methusaleh and Enoch in the bottom row, and Abraham, Hezekiah and David with his harp in the row above.

St. Augustine's Chair

8 THE QUIRE

Passing through the 15th century iron gates under the Pulpitum Screen the full length of the Gothic Quire and Trinity Chapel stretch before us with the **High Altar** standing at the top of a flight of steps and, above that, the marble **St Augustine's chair** (dating, probably, from the 13th century), in which the archbishops have been enthroned as Primates of all England.

After the great fire of 1174 the Quire was rebuilt out of the ruins of its Romanesque predecessor by a French architect, William of Sens, who produced this sensational Gothic design. We can but admire . . . the stone vaulting with its ribs and bosses overhead, the arcades of pointed arches with delicate carving, the shafts of Purbeck marble contrasting with Caen stone, the many stained glass windows especially the Roses of the transepts and above all, the apsidal (semi-circular) east end which recalls the contemporary cathedrals of France.

Cathedral from the south west

In the vault, over the **brass lectern** of 1663, is a boss with the Lamb and Flag, emblem of Our Lord's Resurrection upon it. While building work was in progress at this point, the scaffolding collapsed, throwing William of Sens to the ground. As a result of this severe accident in 1178 he returned to die in Paris and was succeeded by William, the Englishman, who completed the building.

The Resurrection Boss

Worthy of note are the six tombs of the archbishops on each side of the Presbytery, the **stalls of the Cathedral Canons** at the west end carved by Roger Davis in 1682 and the tall spire of the archiepiscopal throne of 1844. In 1985 the quire was 'reseated' with 130 cushions embroidered with coats of arms of dignitaries of the diocese, the work of the Guild and others.

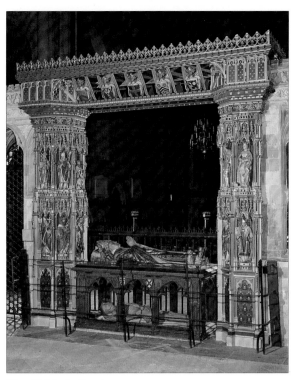

The Chichele Tomb

9 THE NORTH AMBULATORY AND TRANSEPT

Passing into the north transept by the 'double decker' tomb of Archbishop Chichele (died 1443) turn left into the north aisle. Here is Frank Salisbury's painting of a royal visit to the Cathedral in 1946, and a painting of King Charles I (the Martyr) dating from the Restoration c1660.

The two windows of early Gothic glass, dating from around 1200, are part of a lost series known as the 'Bible of The Poor'. Here are the panels showing the Three Kings with parallel scenes from the Old Testament. The second window has roundels showing the Child Jesus in the Temple, the Miracle at Cana, the Miraculous Draught of Fishes and the calling of Nathanael from under the fig tree.

The Sower Panel

In a little gallery above are three small windows with scenes from the lives of the Saxon archbishops, Saint Dunstan and Saint Alphege – all early 13th century, and in embrasure a large mediaeval wall painting, c1480, of the legend of St Eustace, patron saint of hunting.

On returning to the north-east transept more old glass can be seen in the Rose window in the gable of the transept symbolising the Old Testament. The chapels below are dedicated to Saint Martin and Saint Stephen. In the first hangs a 15th century picture of the Saxon queen Ediva, a benefactor of the monastery.

Passing the Victorian monument of Archbishop Howley and the huge tomb of Cardinal Archbishop Bourchier we come to the Norman chapel of **Saint Andrew,** whose vaulted roof and walls are covered with mediaeval paintings, recently restored. An ancient door with three locks leads to the Norman vestiarum c1160 – the vestry of the Cathedral clergy.

10A THE TRINITY CHAPEL

Ascending the pilgrim steps we see, in the first window of the Chapel, a figure of Saint Thomas in mitre and chasuble, thought to be of the late 12th century. It recalls the long association of this Chapel with the Martyr of Canterbury who said his first mass as priest in the Cathedral on Trinity Sunday 1162. All around are a series of windows, which, in vivid glass of the 13th century, record events in which Saint Thomas brought help or healing to those who prayed to him in need. Many panels show the tomb in the crypt where he was first buried, and one or two picture the famous shrine later built here in 1220. Stand at the east end of the chapel and look down over the **site of the shrine,** now marked out by an inscription in brass and a burning candle.

Overhead, in the vaulting, can be seen a crescent of gilded wood thought to have been a votive offering brought from Palestine by the Crusaders after the capture of Acre in the time of Richard the Lionheart. The pavement of this chapel, which culminates at the west end in a mosaic floor made in Rome in the 13th century is one of the finest of its kind in England. A series of roundels, including signs of the zodiac, of French origin, are set on either side of the mosaic behind the marble St. Augustine's chair.

The Thomas Panel

Tomb of Henry IV and Joan of Navarre

Interspersed among the marble pillars, green and pink in colour with carved capitals, are the tombs of royal and ecclesiastical personages, most of whom were buried here in the Middle Ages. They survived when the famous shrine was destroyed by the order of King Henry VIII in 1538. On the north side is the tomb of King Henry IV and his Queen, Joan of Navarre. Opposite is their Chantry Chapel of Saint Edward the Confessor entered through a 15th century wooden screen. In a Renaissance tomb in the next bay lies the first Dean Nicholas Wooton (1542-1567) while a modern cenotaph with a bronze effigy commemorates Archbishop Davidson (died 1930).

11 THE CORONA

This early Gothic chapel was added after the completion of the Trinity Chapel to enshrine a relic – the corona or top of the head of Saint Thomas struck off by one of the assassins – hence its name. It was furnished again and rededicated to the **Saints and Martyrs of our own time** in 1978 at the closing service of the Lambeth Conference.

On his visit to Canterbury in May 1982 Pope John Paul II with Archbishop Runcie and leaders of the religious communities in England came here in procession to light candles in memory of the principal saints and martyrs of their respective denominations.

The altar, vested in a rich modern frontal stands on a mediaeval platform in which are many encaustic tiles. Behind, in the centre of the wall framed among pillars of Purbeck marble, is the 13th century Redemption window which shows scenes of the Crucifixion, Entombment, Resurrection and Ascension of Our Lord with Pentecost at the summit, and small scenes from the Old Testament attached to each New Testament panel.

On the north side is the simple tomb of the last Cardinal Archbishop, Reginald Pole, who died in 1558, while a rugged granite memorial opposite recalls Archbishop Frederick Temple (died 1903) with a bronze effigy of the Archbishop kneeling in prayer, work of F W Pomeroy.

The Corona

The Black Prince's Effigy

10b THE TRINITY CHAPEL SOUTH SIDE

Returning to the Trinity Chapel we move west. The curious brick tomb is that of Cardinal Odet de Coligny, a French nobleman who abjured the Catholic faith to become a Huguenot and died suddenly in Canterbury while on a mission to Queen Elizabeth I to secure help for his co-religionists. Temporarily buried here (with maximum economy) it seems probable that his remains will never return to France.

The oldest tomb in the Cathedral, that of Archbishop Walter (1205) stands under one of the windows, a series of carved heads along its front. Easily the most famous tomb in the building is that of **Edward Prince of Wales** who died in 1376. His effigy shows him in full armour (gilded) on a tomb chest with his black shield with three ostrich feathers, above which hang modern copies of his funeral "achievements". The originals are now in a case at the bottom of the steps where we now proceed.

Original Achievements

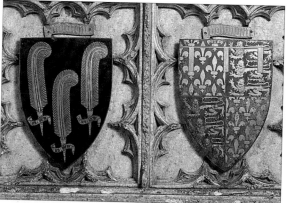

Shields, Black Prince's Tomb

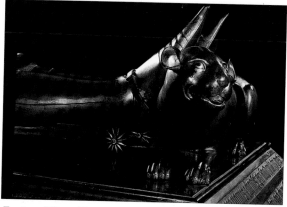

Feet and Dog, Black Prince's Tomb

Opposite this we see the chapel of **Saint Anselm,** a Norman structure in which the great monk Archbishop was buried in 1109. In the apse where the altar stands is a 12th century wall painting of Saint Paul at Malta, shaking off the viper. A modern window in Anselm's honour fills the south wall, the work of Harry Stammers. The black marble tomb of Archbishop Meopham (1333) with contemporary iron gates forms a screen to the Chapel.

The three tombs in this aisle are all of mediaeval archbishops, that nearest the steps being the resting place of Simon of Sudbury, killed in the Peasants' Revolt of 1381. He was beheaded by the mob on Tower Hill at the time of the Watt Tyler rebellion for being, as chancellor, responsible for the hated poll tax. His head is still preserved in the church of Saint Gregory in his native town in Suffolk, while the substitute here takes the form of a ball of lead.

In the south-east transept are chapels of Saint John and Saint Gregory, dedicated today to the memory of Archbishop William Temple and his successor, Geoffrey Fisher. The four windows in the south wall were filled with glass in the 1950s, by Ervin Bossanyi, a Hungarian refugee. The last tomb to note in the Cathedral is that of Henry of Eastry showing him in mitre and chasuble, the only Prior of Canterbury to be buried in like manner to an archbishop. The great screen surrounding the quire dates from his term of office 1285-1331.

A few feet away from this is a Romanesque arcade which escaped the fire. One of the semi-circular arches has been recarved by a mason subsequently. He has pointed the arch and decorated it with characteristic early Gothic dogtooth ornament, perhaps to demonstrate to the monks the new style to be introduced. If we look from here down the nave with its soaring Gothic arches we can see the three main styles of architecture so wonderfully embodied in this mighty church.

As we leave the Cathedral through the south-west door we pass once more the Warriors' Chapel and, on our right, the gift stall.

12 A WALK ROUND THE EXTERIOR

If on leaving the cathedral we turn left we find ourselves walking through some fine lawns and gardens which make up the south side of the Precincts. This has always been a public area separated until the last century by a Romanesque Gateway which led to the monks' enclosed area and their cemetery. This Gate was moved in 1840 further east and now leads into the Kent County War Memorial garden. On the far side of this is a chapel within one of the bastions of the mediaeval city wall which runs along this side of the Precincts. In the corner of this wall is a small door which leads into the street outside, known as the Queningate, since, traditionally, Queen Bertha (c600) used to go this way to her devotions in the little church of Saint Martin before the coming of Saint Augustine and his monks.

Large and impressive houses, formerly occupied by the canons in the north side of this area are now boarding houses for the pupils of the King's School. A fine 17th century house is used by the Cathedral choir boys who also use the 14th century Table Hall of the

Bell Harry Tower

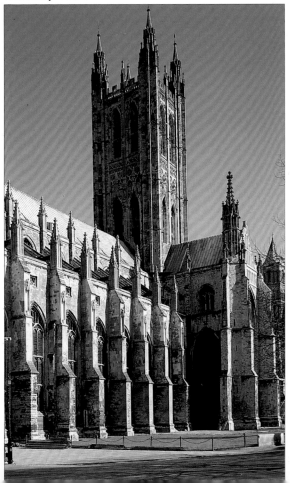

monks' infirmary whose ruined remains are a conspicuous sight along the side of the Cathedral. Passing down the Brick Walk, where the ghost of Nell Cook is said to walk at 9 pm on Friday nights, we turn right at the doorway and go through a dark passage to the **Prior's Gatehouse** which looks across the **Green Court** on the north side of the Precincts.

The buildings here consist of the **Deanery** on the right, with its Tudor facade, and mediaeval buildings ahead once the **Granary, Bakery** and **Brewery** of the monastery, the latter now used by the King's School. In the far corner is the **Great Staircase**, once part of the monastic Almonry, and then comes the Court Gate leading into the Mint Yard and so to the city outside.

Turning back through the Prior's Gatehouse we come to the **Cathedral Library,** rebuilt after being bombed in 1942. The **Water Tower** stands close by, a Romanesque gem once the centre of the monastic water supply. The same supply is still in being, carrying water through ancient pipes from a conduit house outside the city walls to various taps round the Precincts.

We pass through **the Dark Entry** into the **Great Cloister** rebuilt c1400, a quadrangular arrangement of walks round a central garth; the vaulted roofs are studded with more than 800 coats of arms representing the generous benefactors who made the rebuilding of an older cloister possible during the reign of King Henry IV.

On the east side is the monastic **Chapter House**, largest of its kind in England, a great rectangular structure with a lofty oak roof and a noble seat for the Prior who would have presided here daily over the morning assembly of the monks. The two huge windows show characters in the history of the Cathedral (east) and incidents in which they took part (west), in stained glass c1900. Making our way along the north alley of the cloister we pass the door leading into the Archbishop's Palace through which, according to tradition, Becket came to the Cathedral in the winter evening of December 29th 1170 hotly pursued by the knights, who were to murder him within a few minutes.

The Cloister

As we look up at the coats of arms of kings and archbishops of mediaeval times we shall also see on the vault in the south-west corner the arms of Pope John Paul II, Archbishop Robert Runcie and Charles, Prince of Wales, carved and painted there in 1982 to commemorate the great event of May 29th linking history past with history present.

The Old Palace, whose gates we now see as we leave the cloisters is a comparatively modern house embodying

Cathedral from the south west floodlit

some remains of the ancient palace of Archbishops; the Romanesque foundations, going back to Lanfranc's time, have recently been uncovered.

After its destruction, during the Puritan regime, archbishops had no permanent home in their own cathedral city until the rebuilding c1900. Since then successive archbishops have played a considerable part in the life of the cathedral and city.

A mail order service is available. Please call us for a brochure or contact
mailorder@cathedral-enterprises.co.uk
www.cathedral-enterprises.co.uk

The Georgian first floor gallery features local original fine arts and crafts amongst a selection of interesting replicas and other items.

All profits go towards the upkeep of the Cathedral.

Service times

Sundays

Holy Communion	8.00am
Matins said *(or sung by the King's School)*	9.30am
Sung Eucharist*	11.00am
Choral Evensong	3.15pm
Evening Service*	6.30pm

* with Sermon

Weekdays

Holy Communion	8.00am
Wednesday	11.00am
Thursday	6.15pm
Major Saints' Day (Sung)	10.15am

Matins

Monday to Friday	7.30am
Saturday	9.30am

Choral Evensong — 5.30pm
Choral Evensong is at 3.15pm on Saturdays.

Information correct at time of going to press November 2000

Published by Cathedral Enterprises Ltd., Canterbury, England ©
Printed by J. Salmon Ltd., Sevenoaks, Kent, England
ISBN 0 906211 33 6